Movie Science

by Sam Brelsfoard

PEARSON
Scott
Foresman

Sound is a form of energy that travels in waves. Sound is produced when objects vibrate. When sound vibrations travel through air, they cause the air particles to form a pattern. The area of the wave where the particles are bunched together is a compression.

Some waves move in transverse waves. Sound moves in longitudinal waves. The frequency of a wave is the number of waves that pass a point in a certain amount of time. The faster the wave moves, the higher the frequency is. A wavelength is the distance between a point on one wave and a similar point on the next wave. Sound can move through solids, liquids, and gases. Sound cannot move through a vacuum, or empty space.

One characteristic of sound is loudness. Loudness measures how strong a sound seems. Pitch is another characteristic. Pitch is what makes a sound seem high or low. Objects that vibrate slowly have a low pitch, and those that vibrate quickly have a high pitch. Musical instruments can produce sounds with different pitches.

Light is also energy that moves in waves. White light passing through a prism splits into the colors of the visible spectrum. Radio waves, microwaves, and infrared waves are invisible light waves.

Light reflection occurs when light rays bounce off a surface. Absorption occurs when an object takes in light, and the light becomes heat energy.

A transparent material lets light rays pass through it. A translucent material lets only some light rays pass through. An opaque material does not let any light rays pass through.

Light bends when it moves at an angle from one medium to another. This bending is called refraction. Lenses are curved pieces of glass or plastic that refract light that passes through them. Light bends toward the middle of a convex lens. Light spreads out when it passes through a concave lens.

Light and sound energy can be used in many ways. In this book, you will learn about an entertaining use for light and sound—movies!

Prisms split white light into different colors.

Light Pictures

The technology needed for making the movies we see today would not have been possible without the invention of the camera. A camera lens takes in beams of light that bounce off objects. The beams bend as they enter the lens, and an upside-down image is projected onto the camera's film. Chemicals in the film react to light and form an image.

By reversing the process of taking a photograph, an image can be projected on a screen. To do this, light is shone through the film and then through a lens. The lens projects the image from the film onto a screen.

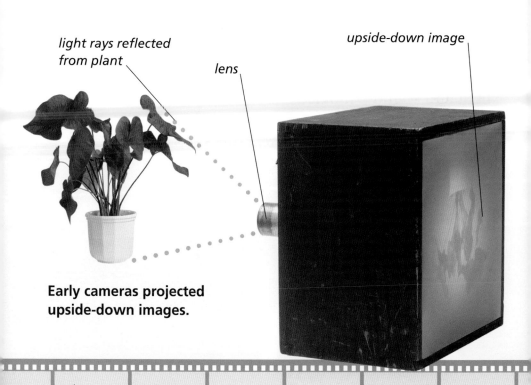

light rays reflected from plant

lens

upside-down image

Early cameras projected upside-down images.

The magic lantern was invented in the 1600s. Images were drawn and painted by hand on small pieces of glass. The magic lantern projected these images onto a large screen using light from an oil lamp.

Toward the end of the 1800s, the magic lantern was being used to entertain huge crowds in the United States. The hand-drawn pieces of glass were replaced with photographs. For many years, this was the only kind of projection equipment available. As photography became more popular, it became easier to produce these images. Eventually motion pictures, or movies, took the place of the magic lantern.

Magic lanterns provided early picture shows.

Images in Motion

When you watch a movie, what you are really watching is a series of thousands of images flickering in front of your eyes. This rapid flickering happens so quickly that you do not see each individual image. Your brain puts the images together. You see the illusion of movement on the screen. This illusion is known as animation. This technology was used in many devices in the nineteenth century. One of these devices was known as the praxinoscope.

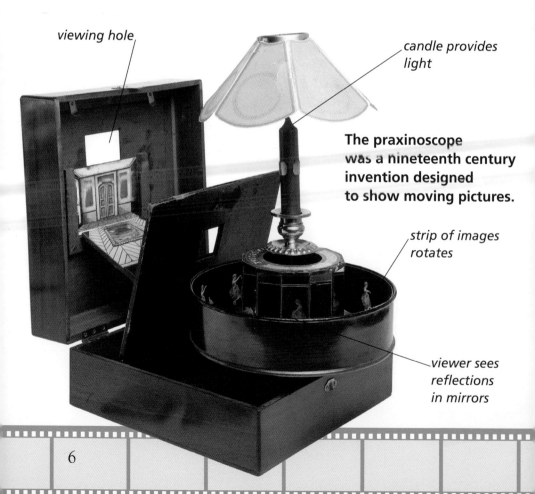

viewing hole

candle provides light

The praxinoscope was a nineteenth century invention designed to show moving pictures.

strip of images rotates

viewer sees reflections in mirrors

How to make a flip book

Take a small stack of paper. On the top page, draw a picture you would like to animate, such as a bird in the sky. On the next page, draw the same picture but make it slightly different. The bird could be in a different position on this page. After you've drawn on each page in the stack, flip through the pages very quickly. The picture will seem to move!

The praxinoscope was a device that produced images that seemed to move. It had a short, wide tube that revolved. On the inside wall of the tube was a series of images. In the middle of the tube was a series of mirrors. The number of mirrors in the praxinoscope equaled the number of images. As the tube rotated, the drawings passed in front of the mirrors. When the tube spun fast enough, the images seemed to move. A candle above the tube supplied light. The viewer looked through a hole on one side to see the series of images forming an animation.

This technology would soon merge with the technology of cameras. This led to the invention of cameras that could record movement.

Movie Cameras

The first movie cameras were surprisingly small and lightweight. The film in a movie camera winds from one reel onto another reel. Film is a long strip of very strong, thin plastic that is coated with light-sensitive chemicals. The film is threaded through the camera. It is guided by sprockets. Sprockets are gearlike wheels. Their teeth fit into the small holes along the sides of the film. Many early cameras, including the Debrie Parvo camera, used a crank to turn the film once it was threaded.

The Debrie Parvo camera was used by many filmmakers in the early 1900s.

crank

simple lens

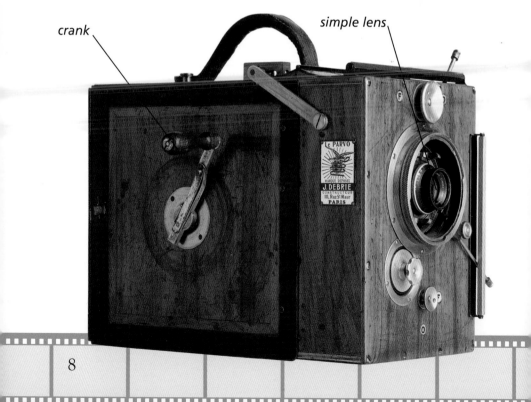

How cameras work

A shutter is a device on a camera that opens and closes. It controls how much light comes through the lens. When the shutter closes, a claw moves forward and catches the holes on the side of the film. This pulls the film down. The shutter then opens again.

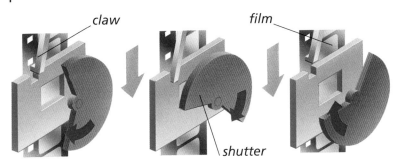

claw   film

shutter

Rotating sprockets move the film through the camera. The film passes in front of the lens. The film is divided into sections called frames. A shutter opens as each frame passes in front of the lens. When the shutter opens, light can reach the film. Twenty-four images per second are captured on the film. Just as you saw in the flip book, each image is slightly different than the one that came before it. This causes the illusion of movement.

frame

sprocket hole

At the Movies

A modern film projector in a movie theater uses very powerful electric lamps to generate light. The projector uses sprockets to push and pull the film, just as a movie camera does. The film passes in front of the shutter. Light shines through it, and images are projected onto a screen.

Projectors have many parts. The lamphouse holds the light source. The images are projected through the lens. The spool cover holds the reels of film.

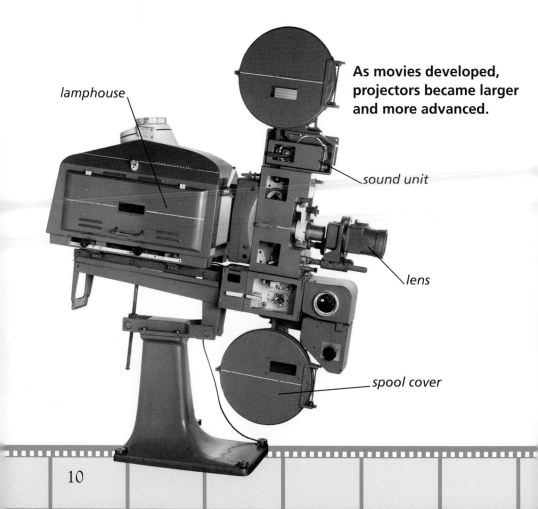

lamphouse

As movies developed, projectors became larger and more advanced.

sound unit

lens

spool cover

How a projector works

Inside a movie projector, a light beam shines past the shutter through a moving strip of film. The lens projects the series of images onto a screen.

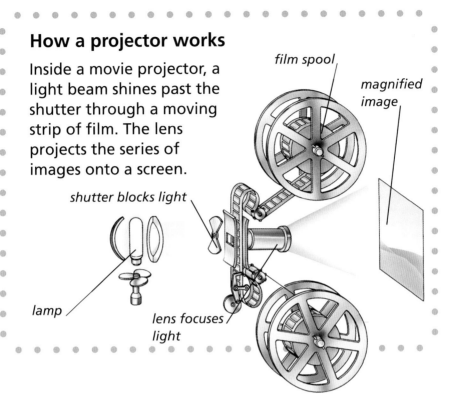

film spool

magnified image

shutter blocks light

lamp

lens focuses light

A strip of film holds more than just the images it has recorded. It often contains the sound for the movie as well. The sound is located on the side of the film next to the images. A sound unit on the projector picks up the sounds. It changes the sound information into electrical signals and sends them out to the speakers in the movie theater. The speakers turn those signals into the sound that you hear. Because the sound information and the images are on the same piece of film, you hear the sound and see the images at the same time.

Cinema in Color

The primary colors of light are red, blue, and green. When you mix these colors in specific amounts, you can make any other color you want. White light is all colors of the visible spectrum put together. In order for movie cameras to properly record the images in front of them, the film must be able to record all of the right color information. Modern movie cameras use film with layers of chemicals that are sensitive to red, blue, and green light. This ensures that the camera will record every color combination of light that enters the lens.

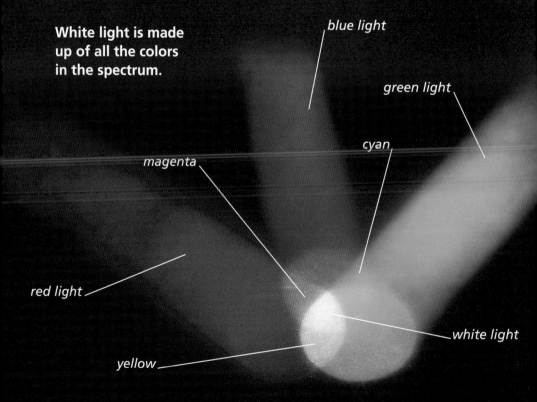

White light is made up of all the colors in the spectrum.

blue light

green light

cyan

magenta

red light

white light

yellow

Early film cameras were not able to record different colors. So the movies they recorded were black and white. Soon the technology became available to make movies in color. Some of the first color cameras that were invented used a prism to record all of the color information on the film. When white light enters a prism, it splits into all its different colors. The prism in the camera caused light to split and enter the lens as three separate colors: red, blue, and green. Each color was put on its own reel of film. In order to show the film in theaters, the colors had to be combined again. The three rolls of film were processed to make one final full-color reel that could be projected with regular projectors.

Early color cameras recorded colors using a prism.

Sound

Sound engineers are the people on a movie set who record the actors' voices, as well as any other sound that is in the movie. The engineers use a large, powerful microphone to capture sound. The sound is then saved on a portable recording device. Usually when engineers are recording sound on a movie set, they will put the microphone at the end of a long mechanical arm called a boom. This keeps the microphone out of the view of the camera while still recording the necessary sounds. Sometimes, if the sound the engineers are trying to capture comes from something that moves throughout the scene, they use a hand-held microphone. This is a microphone that is attached to the end of a pole. It is moved to follow the sound source.

Sound is sometimes recorded with a hand-held microphone.

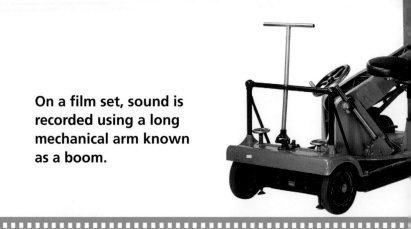

On a film set, sound is recorded using a long mechanical arm known as a boom.

Microphones pick up sound waves in the air and change them into electric signals. These sound signals travel through wires in the microphone to the sound engineers' portable recording device. There they are stored. Later they are carefully lined up with the images that the camera has recorded.

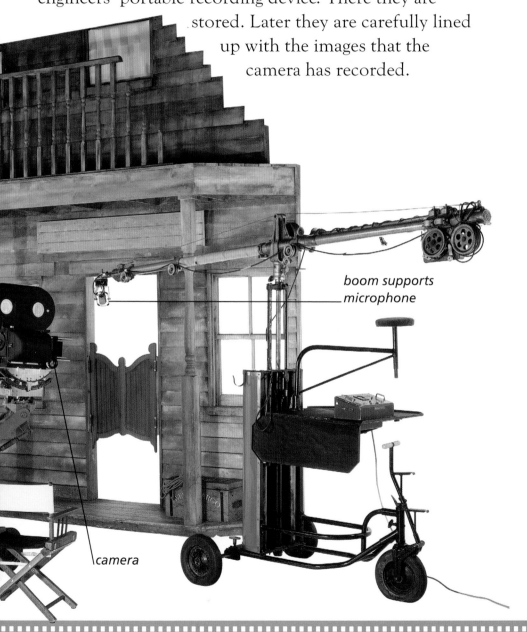

boom supports microphone

camera

Mixing Sound

Most movies have many sounds: dialogue, sound effects, music, and background noises. All of these sounds must be combined to play along with the movie. Usually each sound is recorded separately. What the actors say, the dialogue, is recorded on the set during filming or later in a sound studio. The background sounds can be recorded with or without the actors being present. The sound effects are usually recorded after the scene has been filmed. The music for the movie is often the last part to be recorded.

Dialogue recorded after filming is called a voice-over.

The audio technician sits at a control panel to put together the final sound for the film.

Once all the sounds have been recorded, it is the work of the audio technicians to mix the sounds together. They use special audio equipment to do this. The technicians' main job is to adjust the volume and quality of the sound to make it work well with the movie. They make sure that all the sounds are heard at exactly the right moments.

When the technicians have finished mixing the sounds, they record the complete, final version. This is then added to the side of the final version of the film as a series of magnetic stripes. When the film is played in movie theaters, the sound and the images match up.

Editing the Film

Once all of the movie has been filmed and all of the sound has been recorded, the director and the film editor must edit the film. Often, the scenes in a movie have been filmed out of order. This means that when filming is completed, the director and editor have many rolls of film that must be placed in the right order to make the movie.

Film editors once used a machine called a film splicer.

Today film is fed into computers and edited digitally.

Sometimes many different versions of the same scenes are recorded. The director and the editor spend many hours watching the film and choosing the best versions from what they recorded. They put the scenes in order, cut out the unnecessary parts, and assemble the film. When they are finished, a new roll of film is made that holds the final version of the movie. It is wound onto spools and sent to theaters.

Today computers are used to edit films. Unedited film is fed into a computer. Editors can use the computer to change the film however they wish. The use of computers is a relatively new tool in editing. In the past, editors worked with the actual pieces of film. In order to cut a scene, an editor used a film splicing machine. This machine cut the film at the desired spot and reconnected the pieces that were left. The editors then threw away the unwanted pieces of film. This was a very time-consuming process. Computers make it much easier for editors and directors to edit their movies.

The final film is wound onto spools.

Animation

An animated film contains thousands of drawings. In early animated movies, every drawing that you saw on the screen had been drawn by hand. Every scene in an animated movie is carefully planned before any drawing is done. To reduce the amount of drawing each artist has to do, scenes are planned where the backgrounds stay the same. The detailed background is drawn once, and the animated characters are placed on top of it. To do this, the characters that will be placed on top of the background are drawn on a clear piece of film known as a cel. Each action that the character makes is drawn on a fresh cel. The cels are then placed on top of the background and photographed individually. When the film is played back it looks as if the character and the background are the same drawing. The different layers of animation help make the film appear three-dimensional, or 3-D, instead of flat and two-dimensional. It looks more realistic.

Animation is made up of many layers.

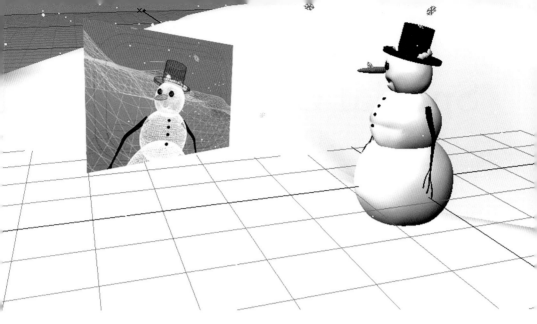

Many animated movies now use computers to create 3-D digital animation.

Most of today's animated films are made using computers. Much of the drawing is done on computers, so animators are free to concentrate on other areas of the film. This does not mean that computer animation is any easier. It is simply a different approach to an old idea. Computer animators are skilled technicians who understand the many uses of very advanced software that can help them make animated movies.

Special Effects

New technology is being developed in the movie industry every day. The blue screen is a technique that caught people's attention when it was first invented. By filming characters in front of a large blue screen, movie editors can later replace the image of the blue screen in the background with anything they want. By replacing the blue screen with stars and planets, for example, filmmakers can make it seem as though characters are flying through space. This sort of technology allows us to see things that seem impossible.

Blue screens enable many special effects.

People have been going to the movies for many years. What will movies of the future be like?

Many films use computer-generated imagery, or CGI, to make special effects. CGI can be used to make it seem as if one character turns into another. Combining CGI and regular film footage can make it seem as though almost anything were possible.

The way we make and watch movies changes all the time. Computers and special effects have changed the way films are made. Digital projectors and DVDs are changing the way we watch movies. We can only guess what's in store for the future of moviemaking. One thing we can count on is that the science behind moviemaking will keep developing and changing to make movies even more entertaining.

Glossary

animation   the production of the illusion of moving images

blue screen   technology in which subjects are filmed in front of a blue-colored screen that can be replaced with other images

boom   a mechanical arm that holds a microphone

cel   a clear piece of film on which a character is drawn and then placed over a background illustration

praxinoscope   an early device that gave the illusion of images in motion

shutter   part of a camera that opens and closes to control how much light comes through the lens

splicing   joining two objects together, such as pieces of film

sprockets   gearlike wheels with teeth that fit into the small holes on the sides of film